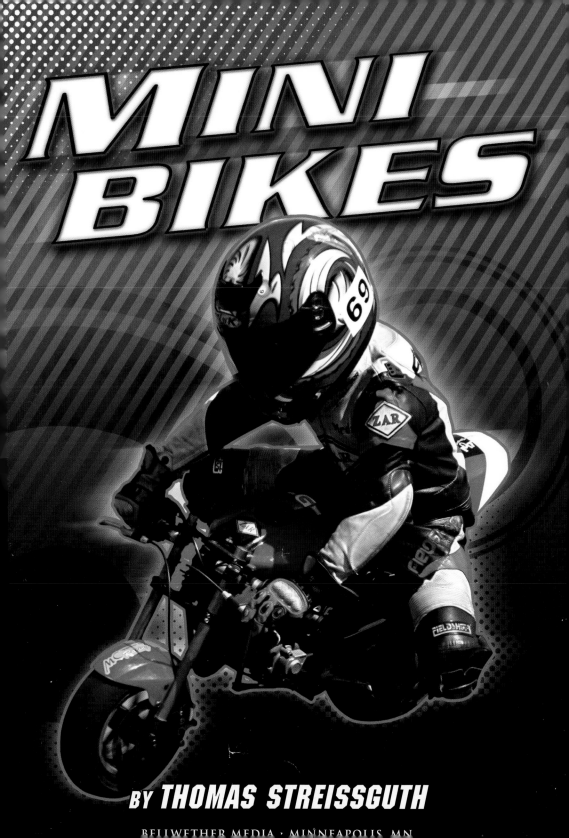

MINI BIKES

BY **THOMAS STREISSGUTH**

BELLWETHER MEDIA · MINNEAPOLIS, MN

TM

Are you ready to take it to the extreme?
Torque books thrust you into the action-packed
world of sports, vehicles, and adventure.
These books may include dirt, smoke, fire, and
dangerous stunts.
WARNING: Read at your own risk.

Library of Congress Cataloging-in-Publication Data

Streissguth, Thomas, 1958–
  Mini Bikes / by Thomas Streissguth.
    p. cm. – (Torque–motorcycles)
  Summary: "Full color photography accompanies engaging information about mini bikes.
The combination of high-interest subject matter and light text is intended for students in
grades 3 through 7"–Provided by publisher.
  Includes bibliographical references and index.
  ISBN-13: 978-1-60014-155-3 (hardcover : alk. paper)
  ISBN-10: 1-60014-155-2 (hardcover : alk. paper)
  I. Title.

TL443.S768 2008
629.227'5–dc22   2007040743

CONTENTS

WHAT IS A
MINI BIKE?

Mini bikes are miniature motorcycles designed for fun. They are tiny, fast, and exciting. They can do almost anything a full-size motorcycle can. Riders race them around both paved and dirt courses. Some weigh as little as 50 pounds (22.7 kilograms)!

Mini bikes have been around since the 1950s. The first ones were built in garages. People built frames out of spare parts. They attached small engines. Professional racing teams started to use them for moving around **pit areas**. The teams needed small, fast vehicles to help quickly refuel **stock cars** and **dragsters**.

FAST FACT

BAFFLES ARE USED TO MUFFLE THE NOISE OF A MINI BIKE ENGINE. HOWEVER, MANY RACERS REMOVE THE BAFFLES DURING RACES TO GET MORE ENGINE POWER. MEMBERS OF THE CROWD OFTEN WEAR EARPLUGS FOR PROTECTION FROM THE LOUD NOISE.

Mini bikes have been popular since the 1970s. Some kids race them on go-kart tracks or in abandoned parking lots. Many young people ride them off-road. Because mini bikes are so small, they're not legal on streets or sidewalks.

MINI BIKE FEATURES

Mini bikes have lightweight parts. Their frames are built of **aluminum**. Aluminum weighs much less than steel. Most mini bikes have **two-stroke** engines. The top speed on most mini bikes is around 50 miles (80.5 kilometers) per hour. Gas tanks hold about a half-gallon (1.9 liters) of fuel. Mini bikes can get more than 100 miles (161 kilometers) per gallon.

Other features make operating a mini bike easy. An **automatic transmission** gives a smooth ride. **Foot pegs** allow the rider to remain stable on the bike. Rear **coil shocks** cushion hard bumps. Riders can adjust handlebar and seat height to suit their needs. Some mini bike parts are just for decoration. Riders can "trick out" their mini bikes with modified seats and handlebars.

FAST FACT

MOTORCYCLE MANUFACTURERS SUCH AS THUMPSTER, PITSTER PRO, AND MOTOVERT ALL MAKE MINI BIKES. EVEN HARLEY-DAVIDSON, THE MOST FAMOUS AMERICAN MOTORCYCLE COMPANY, MADE A MINI BIKE IN THE 1970S. THEY CALLED IT "THE SHORTSTER."

Mini bike riders always wear a helmet for protection. Riders also wear gloves and kneepads. Knees can easily scrape the ground in a tight turn. A wipeout on a mini bike can be just as dangerous as on a full-size motorcycle.

MINI BIKES
IN ACTION

Mini bikes come in different styles for different types of riding. **Pit bikes** are miniature dirt bikes. They have bigger engines and tougher frames than standard mini bikes. Pit bikes have knobby tires that can handle rough surfaces. Riders take pit bikes up steep hills, on muddy trails, and even over jumps.

Pocket bikes are mini bikes built for adults. They are used for racing. Their engines pack a lot of power.

Some can reach speeds of over 70 miles (112.7 kilometers) per hour. Only experienced riders should take on these racing machines.

The popularity of mini bikes has resulted in manufacturers making mini ATVs. The miniaturized all terrain vehicles give a stable ride over the roughest terrain. Miniature machines continue to grow in popularity. They offer big fun in a small package.

FAST FACT

YOU NEED A LICENSE TO RIDE A MINI BIKE IN SOME STATES. SOME STATES ALSO HAVE MINIMUM-AGE REQUIREMENTS ON RIDERS. RIDERS MUST CHECK WITH THE DEPARTMENT OF MOTOR VEHICLES IN THEIR STATE TO LEARN THE LAWS.

GLOSSARY

aluminum–a strong, lightweight metal

automatic transmission–a part of an engine that automatically changes gears according to the speed of a vehicle

coil shocks–parts of a vehicle designed to cushion a bumpy ride; coil shocks look like springs.

dragsters–racing vehicles made to have extremely quick acceleration down a straight track

foot pegs–small pegs on which the rider rests his or her feet for control and balance of a mini bike

pit area–the area on a racetrack where cars go to fuel up, change tires, and make minor repairs

pit bikes–mini bikes made for rough, hilly terrain

pocket bikes–mini bikes made for adults

stock cars–racing cars based on factory models; stock cars are modified for high-speed racing.

two-stroke–the fuel-burning part of the engine cycle; the number of strokes tells how many times a metal rod called a piston moves in each cycle.

TO LEARN MORE

AT THE LIBRARY

David, Jack. *Enduro Motorcycles*. Minneapolis, Minn.: Bellwether, 2008.

Pupeza, Lori. *Mini Bikes*. Edina, Minn.: Abdo, 1999.

Streissguth, Thomas. *Pocket Bikes*. Minneapolis, Minn.: Bellwether, 2008.

ON THE WEB

Learning more about motorcycles is as easy as 1, 2, 3.

1. Go to www.factsurfer.com

2. Enter "motorcycles" into search box.

3. Click the "Surf" button and you will see a list of related web sites.

With factsurfer.com, finding more information is just a click away.

INDEX

The images in this book are reproduced through the courtesy of: Roslina binti Yusoff,
front cover, 19; Michael Doolittle/Alamy, pp. 5, 6, 8, 11, 12, 14, 17; KTM Sportmotorcycle
AG, p. 15; Andrea Leone, p. 18; American Honda Motor Co., p. 20.